HEARTS & MINDS

BY

MARIA V A JOHNSON

Copyright © 2012 Maria V A Johnson

License Notes

Maria V A Johnson has asserted her rights under the Copyright, Designs and Patents Act 1998 to be identified as the author of this work.

This book is sold subject to the condition that it may not be resold, hired out, be lent or otherwise circulated without the author's prior consent in any form of binding or cover other than that in which it was published and without a similar condition, including this condition, being imposed on the subsequent purchaser. Thank you for respecting the hard work of this author.

ISBN-13: 978-1-939296-68-9

ISBN-10: 1939296684

Myrddin Publishing Group

Credits:

Editor: Shaun Allan

Cover: Ceri Clark

Contact us at: www.myrddinpublishing.com

Acknowledgements

No author is an island. There is always someone who has played a part in getting the final version to publication. With this in mind, I would like to thank Shaun Allan, for being a great editor and making me see the flaws in my work. Also my thanks go to Ceri Clark for the beautiful cover design – you've got talent girl! Finally, thanks to Carlie M A Cullen for helping me to put everything together.

Dedication

To my wonderful mother, Carlie, without whom I would never have had the courage to pursue my dreams; and who helped guide me in putting this book together.

Also, to Rebekka, my beautiful twin sister and my guardian angel. Thank you for watching over me, and I wish you could be with me here in the flesh.

Contents

Loss

Memory	3
The Last Day	5
Angels	7
The Chair	9
Mistress	11
Twin Sister	13

Love

Original Sin	17
Together 2006	19
Twilight	21
Affirmation	23
The Couple	24

Lyrical

Enchanted	27
The Night	29
Ode to my Bookcase	31
Summer Day	32
Innocent	35
The Man	36
Summer Sleep	37

Life

Assassin	41
Blackpool	43
Bullied	47
Illusion	49
Party Time	53
Recession	55
Cleaning House	59

Loss

Memory

Smoke coils from the cigarette
clasped between scrawny fingers,
ash floats down, hits the tray.

A film forms over discarded butts,
clings to the crimson lipstick smears
coating the ends.

She drops the stub beside the others.
Where she sits, the ceiling yellowed.
Nails stained by years of addiction,
what harm can be done now?

Relief spirals away with smoke,
she clutches her abdomen tight
against the pain of mutated cells.
Her sight dims, her brain contaminated.

Extracts another from the packet,
she lights it; takes a drag.
"Another one Nanna?"
"What are you talking about?
I haven't had one for ages!"

The Last Day

He lay on his closing bed,
pallid complexion, waxy features
disguise the once handsome face.

The hypodermic transporter timed at intervals
to propel narcotics, respite from agonies
into the slow-collapsing veins.

She gazes with adoration
his Bible in her adolescent hands
open at a favourite marked passage.

Soft melodic voice delivers the belovèd words,
composure belying her tender years
four hours of devotion.

Breath stutters; ragged, uneven.
Each halt grows increasingly longer.
Her heart falters with every wrenching pause.

She embraces the fragile, emaciated figure
whispers of love, unacknowledged
utters her final goodbyes.

Breathing slows,
ceases forever.
Her quiet tears finally fall.

Angels

To my wonderful grandmother. You are sorely missed.

You used to call me your Little Angel,
Now you are one of them,
Your boundless kindness never was met,
And always you were a gem.

Your body always was around me,
Now your spirit is everywhere,
I know I should not mourn your passing,
But it's more than I can bear.

I will not stand at your grave and weep,
For I know the truth,
You are happy where you are,
Though I have no proof.

This is not your resting place,
I will not stand and cry,
For I know you are not there,
And that you did not die.

I know these words can never express,
The love I feel for you,
Yet this is my only chance to say,
Loving you, I was born to do.

The Chair

The chair sits stark and silent,
its occupant gone.
A mass of letters

stacked nearby, no one
there to open them.
A brown patch stains

the ceiling, a stale
smell clings to the fabric -
old smoke.

A spaniel casts its lonely eyes
approaches, sniffs
and slinks away.

Reading glasses discarded
on its arm, blank screen before it,
no haunting strains

of Emmerdale make us
yell for quiet; no better tune
than the one we lost.

Mistress

I sit and wait.
My mistress in the store.
I get up and pace silently,
my sore covered furless skin
is vein blue and sheer,
pain splits my sides.
Strangers leave, I nuzzle
their hands. Lie down panting,
gravel scrapes slivers off my ribs.
Memory stirs, taking a steak
from Mistress long ago
at the beginning.

I wake with the sun
still watching, still waiting.
The strangers pass and stop
look at my collar, dirty and tag-less.
He runs in, returns with water.
I lap gently, lick his hand,
I sit and wait.

Twin Sister

You're forever with me
yet never seen
you make my marrow chill
as if I were in my grave
with you, lying next to me.

Pressure builds like a weight
on my brain as you talk –
or try to.
Tingles dance goosebumps
up my arm as we touch –
then pass through.

I feel you near
but long for your presence
the life we could have had
the fun times together.
My nightmares would cease
my demons would vanish
you would keep me strong
but your absence tears my heart
my guardian angel.

You died before I was born;
yet always I knew you,
before I was told.

My invisible friend,
with me to the end.

Love

Original Sin

The path glittered beside us
yellow, green as we lay
on a bed of pine needles.
My blood pumped hard
through my adolescent body.
I caressed her strong muscled thigh
in the late afternoon sunshine.

The plucked red rose
rested on her bosom,
blood petals strewn around her.
She inhaled its heady scent;
enchanter of the woods.

The apple from the hidden tree
lay discarded and broken.

Must return home,
past Sunday curfew,
she just lies there free
from the rules of society.

My lips brush this unadorned Venus,
savour the taste
of that apple on my lips
and wish I could have it
once more.

Together 2006

In Rome we sit at a table for two,
no hidden corner, the light glares down.

Two glasses rest; one half empty.
Head buzzing.

No soft strains romance us,
Only the cheering football fans,

"Italy wins the World Cup!"
Drivers honk their horns

streamers pop, shower us with tissue.
You reach across, slowly entwine your
fingers

whispers on my face, you pull the tissue free.
Sea-green eyes gaze into mine, a soft smile.

hold out your hand, pay.
You pull me across the road,

race in 3 inch heels, dodge speeding cars,
holding me tight, beneath the stars.

Twilight

She stood alone
on the barren cliffs
the dark forest behind her,
the crashes and clashes below
echoed in her eyes.

A rhythmic thud turns her,
she smiles and he blossoms
into light, his bronze mane
streams wolf-like in the breeze.
Caresses
her hand, watches the waves
break on the quiet shore.
The calm straightens him
from a predatory crouch,
the wolf retreats into the man.

The sun flashes
behind roiling clouds.

She frowns, her heart
turning to the night, a pale face,
a seductive smile,
black locks in his eyes and
an eternally hidden existence
on the lifeblood of nature
with her love in shadows.

Affirmation

Auburn hair gleams

coils down her back

smiles mysteriously, waiting

rich red wood behind

red dress, matching lipstick

he's older than she

cheap tickets – still young

babysitters on tap

reflecting back

time to rediscover.

The Couple

As the sun rose red and gold,
As the stream flowed on its way,
There a man whose heart be bold,
Waited for his love one day,
Their love was pure, their hearts were true,
They could withstand the tests of time,
Joining together, they'd never rue,
Causing their futures to intertwine,
No matter what was said or done,
None could hold that love at bay,
Evil wind the lovers did shun,
At the closing of the day,
When cares are banished far away,
Her beauteous heart holds sway.

Lyrical

Enchanted

Beautiful faces on perfect tiny bodies
ethereal apparel floats effortlessly
around diaphanous fairy wings.

Blossoms spiral into helixes
petals isolate, fashion silhouettes
that waft eternally towards heaven.

Moonlight gallops; pure-bred stallions
cross the Sprite-filled diamond lagoon,
tender waves lick the shore's lips

where exquisite Elves dance.
Small and lonely, they appear
lively yet forlorn, desire new friends.

Boughs shimmer in moon's
countenance
its radiance misting the eyes
of the fauna in the dell.

Petite yet majestic, silver hides
twinkle as stars in the firmament,
at glade's frame, Unicorn foals gambol.

Melodic strands encompass them all
mystical images painted by voices,
Pixie enchantments intertwine.

The Night

To be at sea,
To guard the waves,
To see the starlight play
Among fields of blue and green
Stretching endlessly to the horizon,
As far as the eye can see.

The night at peace,
The creaking hull,
The gentle rocking of the swell,
A child in her mother's arms,
Protected from all harm,
Drifts silently off to sleep.

The sailors aloft,
The perfection of night,
The heavenly beauty of the view,
Fall in love with the mother of all,
Compose lyrical love poems
Whilst waiting out the dawn.

The stars wink out,
The moon seeks her bed,
The first ray of sunlight
Plays across the water,
To this beauty, the child awakes
And the sailors drift off to sleep.

Ode to my Bookcase

Oh beautiful bookcase, carpenter's creation
Delicately detailed in every line
Smoothly sanded to gleam the grain
Huge holder of my prized possessions
Brilliant books of fantasy fiction
Where your mind will wander
Over verdant fields of green.

__Summer Day__

Freshly mown grass surrounds majestic trees
boughs sway, gentle wind whispers through the foliage,
afternoon sun streams down from the azure heavens
turning the emerald canopy golden.

Manicured beds of scented blossoms artfully placed around the vast perimeter,
glorious hues of pastels and brights attract the delicate pollen gatherers.

Mothers seated on benches and blankets
vigilant monitors of their offspring,
attentive yet relaxed as they natter
enjoy the freedom of the day.

Shrieks and giggles as children play
chase and hide, balls of rainbow colours
soar through the air and on the terrain
as games are won or lost.

Small creatures forage in the undergrowth,
search for sustained nourishment
scamper away when people approach
but ever-watchful of their find.

Lovers saunter along winding trails
hands entwined, peals of laughter
in harmony with melodic birdsong.
This day, a perfect existence.

Innocent

Rose petals soft, as a baby's skin
A child's innocence, like burning rays of light
Fire blazes, purifying us,
Like a lightning bolt from Heaven
Fire, cardinal, untameable
Like wolves roaming the land
A ring of roses, like a death omen
The rose fading
Like a lover's death.

The Man

The face of the man, smiling in the sun
His blonde wavy hair, falling in his eye
His muscles ripple, as through sand he runs
Leaving her standing, on the beach to cry.

Summer Sleep

The sun shimmers
ice-cream trucks tinkle,
resemble desert caravans
wavy and indistinct.

Grandpa, red as the tomatoes
growing in the garden
knee deep in clay
watering can in hand
coaxes dying flowers to life.

Nanna, roasting, hotter
than the chicken in the oven,
chops fresh garden vegetables
already wilting in the heat.

I stroke the soft heads
of the sleeping dogs.
Misty golden brown and
Starry black as velvet sky.

My eyelids tremble
I push them over, climb in
curl like a foetus.

In the basket,
with my puppy-dogs,
I fall asleep.

Life

Assassin

Viewpoint - good, hidden.
Line of sight – clear.

Scan the room.
All entrances blocked.

A truck – black, plain.
Men emerge – guards.

Feelings of déjà vu.
Guards always at hand.

Turn away. Leave.
Another opportunity will present.

An ebony shirt.

The colour of death.

Guards search the buildings.

Mark alone. Contract complete.

Blackpool

I see them.
Their first Nationwide Finals
as I remember mine.

The Empress Ballroom,
huge, crowded,
light shining everywhere
refracting from the golden ceiling.
A riot of colour
my shimmering purples
or their black and pink
contrast the day-glo competitors.
Food is ash in my mouth
bats flap in my stomach
swords dig in my throat
I tremble as nerves overtake me.

I see my old fear reflected in them.

I walk on the floor, ready
as the atmosphere overwhelms me
I am strong, confident, shining
on top of the world
my skin tingling
as I take my place
ready to dance
knowing I will never tire
as adrenaline flows through me.

They look nervous yet elegant
a simple suit of black
pink shirt matches polka dot dress
as they take to the polished floor.

Their trembling ceases
the beat of the music
echoes the pounding of their hearts
and their bodies
heave, turn, fly
through the air;
the electricity and
invincibility fills them.

They leave the floor
sweat pouring in rivers
their shoulders slumping
as they pant for a breath
that will not satisfy.

My bones ache and I
feel deep down the
elation of winning
I see in their eyes
as they cross to receive
their glittering trophy.

<u>Bullied</u>

Fear everywhere, surrounding me,
I was the odd one,
the one that wasn't liked,
the outcast,
the victim of the class.

Girls and boys tormented me,
physical was bad,
mental was worse,
only one would help,
one teacher.

The years of hell at school,
torment without end,
that continued at home,
my older step-sisters
hated me.

Eventually I could take no more,
death my only release,
a suicide attempt alerted
Mum to the danger,
took action.

Took me to the head teacher,
laid the truth bare,
and he ended it.
Mum came down heavy
on my sisters.
Helped me to live free.

__Illusion__

It was time to dance
yet I was not there
the team, my dream
dancing without me.

Sitting central
watching, waiting,
hidden tears choking
the alien smile.

My decision to leave for uni
yet still I was there
as close as I could get –
first reserve.

Teacher decreed
"no dancing if injured
reserve is well trained
and can take any place."

Katie was injured, her actions
unfinished, slow, weak.
Her eyes showed the truth
her face did not acknowledge.

She defied the teacher
let the team down
deprived a fitter dancer
an opportunity to shine.

Pain lanced through me
a heat tearing my soul
freezing me to the core –
yet nothing showed.

I comforted them after,
calmed them, waited anxiously
and commiserated with them –
yet still nothing showed.

Only later with the team gone
could I let my restraint go.
My shoulders heaved,
I could barely breathe
as I sobbed into Mum's arms.

She was silent as she hugged me
tightly to her breast
let me spend myself
growing calmer in her arms.

"I'm so proud of you"
she said at last
"you acted so professionally,
but they let you down."

Party Time

Monday night, party time,
straighten hair, slippery as glass
blisters on her hand.

Eyebrows plucked – painful
extension mascara – false
rose-red lips – tacky.

We grab drinks first
lambrini, vodka, wine,
student's budget.

Taxi honks outside
friends pile out,
trip over each other.

I close the door behind them,
climb back up the stairs,
return to my books.

Recession

"Doom, gloom and despondency" *Small Business Owner*

Printer pages glare white where order forms should be,
an inbox of red pages, demands for payment;
out of balance.
She stumbles rushing from pile to phone.

Mortgage debts turn the brown coffee table white,
monthly bills surround the chairs - unmet,
jumble sale clutter gathers dust from pride.

Darkness shrouds the house,
illumination
only the flicker of internet pages, she
searches for options.

Sleepless eyes black from nights spent
in arguments
not ending at the bedroom door.
Constant calls chase money at work, at
home.
Her screams drown the ring.

Worry lines age her young face
daily stress migraines
adds to her terse demeanour
long discarded habits broken
like once elegant nails.
Health deteriorates, food nauseates.

Can't reason, wants to flee
panic attacks steal her breath.
Pills fill her hand, the baby cries,
her hand jerks them into the sink.

The banker sits straight; smiles and nods.
Government rescue package inaccessible.
Shaft suppliers to pay wages
taste of bile fills her mouth.

The printer churns, spits out pages
black with details of orders,
she smiles, runs her fingers
through her hair and sighs.

Black eyes darken
from nights spent to finish each order
in time to invoice,
to pay wages and bills.
Has the nightmare ended?
Or is this
simply a reprieve?

Cleaning House

Every week, by turn
we clean the house.
The lounge I hate.
The lounge I never use.

I tiptoe through the
sweet covered floor,
shiver at the tableau,
the futility of cleaning
ruined in an hour.

Throws from chairs lie in heaps.
Nessie's shoes, kicked off
after another drunken night;
the smell of mouldy cheese
burns my nose.

Make-up on the mirror
smears my reflection.
Rachael's straighteners
turn the green chair black.

Dishes, dirty with leftover
chicken and pasta,
glasses stained red
clutter the tables.

Red blotch on the carpet
stark against the cream
remnants of a drink,
the glass on its side
had spilt its' life's blood.

Half-eaten pizza rests
in its box, smell of pepperoni
curdles my stomach.

More Exciting Titles from
Myrddin Publishing Group

Tower of Bones by Connie J Jasperson

Crown Phoenix: Night Watchman Express by Alison DeLuca

Crown Phoenix: The Devil's Kitchen by Alison DeLuca

Crown Phoenix: Lamplighter's Special by Alison DeLuca

The Ring of Lost Souls by Rachel Tsoumbakos

Silent No More by Krista Hatch

Dark Places by Shaun Allan

Check www.myrddinpublishing.com for new titles coming soon.

Another Gripping Book

Heart Search book one: Lost by Carlie M. A. Cullen

One bite starts it all . . .

When Joshua Grant vanishes days before his wedding his fiancée Remy is left with only bruises, scratch marks and a hastily written note. Heartbroken, she sets off alone to find him and begins a long journey where strange things begin to happen.

As Joshua descends into his new immortal life he indulges his thirst for blood and explores his superhuman strength and amazing new talents while becoming embroiled in coven politics which threaten to destroy him. But Remy discovers a strength of her own on her quest to bring Joshua home.

Fate toys with mortals and immortals alike, as two hearts torn apart by darkness face ordeals which test them to their limits.

Keep your eyes peeled for book two: Found coming in 2013!

Also by Maria V A Johnson

The Other Way is Essex

A Compilation by Writebulb Writers Group

From the well-known commercial centre of Clacton Pier to the hidden treasures of Highwood; see Essex as you have never seen it before. Remember with us, times spent in Essex; and follow us into the realms of historical fiction, as we try to imagine what could really have happened all those years ago. Even follow an Essex girl to Lancaster. What does she really think of the North/South divide?
From the Romans to modern times, from fact to fiction, from prose to poetry, The Other Way is Essex has something for everyone.

Maria V A Johnson is a professional editor and author with a BA Hons Degree in English and Creative Writing. She first started writing seriously, when she wrote a poem for her grandmother's funeral and she grew to love poetry and writing from there. She has collaborated in a book entitled The Other Way is Essex, which raises money for Farleigh Hospice in Chelmsford, Essex not far from her home.

She can be found on her website at:
http://mariavajohnson.com

www.ingramcontent.com/pod-product-compliance
Lightning Source LLC
Chambersburg PA
CBHW071414040426
42444CB00009B/2235